I0202237

Live Through It
Overcoming Isolation,
Domestic Violence, and Abuse

Live Through It: Overcoming Isolation, Domestic Violence, and Abuse
By
Pamela Whitt

Published by Greater Works Publishing
A Division of Greater Works Enterprises, LLC
2016

Copyright © 2016 by Pamela Whitt

All rights reserved. This book or any portion thereof may not be reproduced or used in any manner whatsoever without the express written permission of the publisher except for the use of brief quotations in a book review or scholarly journal.

First Printing: 2016

ISBN 978-0-9975643-0-3

Greater Works Publishing
A Division of Greater Works Enterprises, LLC

Dedication

This book is dedicated to my daddy Mr. David Adams, Sr., a true craftsman by trade with no training. He would visualize whatever it was he was going to build or design the way it supposed to be and do it, just like he saw it. This spoke volumes to me and taught me to fully examine a project before pursuing it. Or as the scripture says "a wise woman will consider a field before she buys it (Prov. 31)". He was a "word" man. He would paint a picture of the word of God throughout the house. He'd say something like "You should be able to see the word in action where ever you are."

My daddy never met a stranger. He would talk to anyone. There was a boldness in him that we all desired. He loved his family and was the protector of his home. We had no worries as children. He was a good example of a hard worker and each of his children became successful business owners; my mother also owns a restaurant and catering service. We were taught that "you can do it!"

He is with the Lord now, and I miss him tremendously. If he were here, he would say "Tell the story Pam, drive it in like a hammer!"

Table of Contents

Chapter 1 – In The Beginning

My life started as a vibrant tomboy, the first child to my parents, a young girl who loved to play two-hand-touch flag football and had to have a boy's bike's, no girly things. I loved the excitement of hot colors and was a daddy's girl who wanted to do everything he did and go everywhere he went. So I had to be tough but eventually turned into a girly girl although I don't really remember when that happened. Now, I'm in love with fashion, cosmetics, perfume, heels and hair!

I was a teen that loved school but just wasn't trying to be the brightest kid in the class doing just enough to make the grade. I was curious about life, and loved to have fun. Being in the marching band was the highlight of my school days; that's where I met the love of my life Eric Whitt. He was always telling jokes and making me laugh. He was after me like the plague and he won me over.

Eric and I dated throughout high school. He was a few grades higher than I and upon graduating he enlisted in the military (U.S. Navy). I accepted his decision to enlist but wasn't really happy about it knowing that I would miss him. When he left for basic training, it was hard to believe he was gone. We couldn't talk like we use to and couldn't see each other; my world was shaken! We had become tight, inseparable and his leaving was hard. After six weeks, he returned home and the excitement was unreal. We spent every waking moment with each other and our families. Then it came time for him to leave; he was being assigned to duty. Neither he nor I knew when and if he would be returning. The thought of that caused my emotions to be everywhere.

A couple of years passed and after finishing school I got pregnant on one of Eric's trips home. I didn't know it for four months because everything flowed as normal but I could feel some physical changes in my body. Telling my best friend what I was experiencing and she said "You're pregnant." I made an appointment with the doctor and behold, I was with child.

Things changed between Eric and me. He would come home but I wasn't the first person he'd notify anymore. He would be home for hours and I wouldn't know it. When it was time for me to deliver the baby, I called his house and his aunt answered the phone. I let her know about the contractions and that I was about to deliver the baby. She said that she would give him the message. Waiting all evening to see him and even ordering dinner at the hospital for him, he never showed. This sent me another message. Another one that said he didn't care. Things were already rocky, and that was it for me. If he didn't want to see his son, I didn't want him to see him. When the baby and I went home Eric came to the house to see the baby, but I wouldn't let him. It was over as far as I was concerned (I didn't find out that he really didn't get the message until years later).

After ending it with Eric, I really felt alone. Comfort was found at my aunt's house. It was easy to talk to her and let her know what I was truly feeling. There I met Michael. He would speak and make small talk. I responded favorably not realizing that he was making a pass. Over a period of time, he told me things that any young lady with a child would want to hear. He had a good job, a house, car and money. He told me how he would love to take care of me and my son and that we wouldn't want for anything. People that knew him warned me that he wasn't the right one for me, but they never said why, and I didn't ask. I thought they were saying that because everyone wanted me to get back together with Eric. Eventually, Michael asked me to marry him and although I was not physically attracted to him, I thought about it. I had a funny feeling all the while, but didn't know what it was until after we said "I do".

Chapter 2 – The Marriage

When Michael first asked me to marry him, I didn't say yes right away. We continued with the dating process and one day at the park, he pulled out a ring and asked the question again. This time I said okay.

We got married at his home and we didn't have a real honeymoon. The whole day of the wedding I had caution or warning signs. When trying to get ready, I couldn't find my purse or my shoes; and we had a flat tire on the way to the wedding. My aunt said to me immediately after the wedding "good luck." Someone else told me "You won't recognize that monster until he rears his head." Then the reflections started. I immediately thought of the day I tried on my wedding dress and my friends come over to do girly things in preparation for the wedding. Michael walked in as asked "What are you doing?" I said "The girls are just about to give me a makeover". He said in a stern voice "I don't want you wearing that stuff." I told the girls don't worry about it meaning not to go any further with the makeup. They all looked at each other in amazement as I tried on that beautiful dress with such a plain face and a flower stuck in my hair. I looked and felt a hot mess. Perhaps if I had stood my ground right then, things would have turned out differently. Somehow I knew that the real Michael was wearing a mask but I was in it too far to turn around.

We're married now and we have two children. Our youngest is a little girl six weeks old. I remember this one particular day which was a Wednesday - this was the day that I looked forward to the most because I would spend the day with my mother. It was her only day off and because Michael isolated me from my family, friends, television, and took the keys to the car, Wednesdays had become most precious to me. I was making breakfast, my son was in his chair in his own little world and the baby girl was in my arms. Michael walked into the kitchen and instead of a warm kiss or a cordial greeting I was being shouted at and accused of cheating. I stood there wondering how? How could I? I was literally cut off from everyone and everything, practically isolated. I tried to ignore the accusation by making small talk, saying "Remember that today is Wednesday and my mother was coming to pick up me and the children." He said "You're not taking my daughter anywhere." He had imagined in his mind that my mom was taking me to see Eric. Eric was nowhere in my thoughts. That was his way of keeping me from my mother. He launched out and grabbed the baby and we tussled over her. She was dangling between the two of us and to prevent her from getting hurt I let go. I told him that the kids and I were going, walked into the bedroom to call my mother and the phone went dead. Michael pulled the phone and the phone jack right out of the wall. I told Michael he can keep his phone and threw the it on the floor and walked pass him. I immediately felt a blow to the back of my head and stumbled forward. I felt his hands around my neck as I fell to the floor. Michael then jumped on my back and began choking the life out of me. I was gasping for breath and as I inhaled his grip got tighter. I couldn't speak out but he could. He said "I will kill your mother f****** a**." I felt my body functions giving away. Everything inside of me felt like it was going down and out. I said in my mind and heart, "Jesus, help me! You've got to help me". All of a sudden, Michael let go. I pushed away and sat there trying to catch my breath, gasping. Michael stooped down on the floor in front of me. He had one hand on his face and the other hand was dangling between his legs looking at me as if he was getting ready for round two. Then he asked if I was going to leave him. I was thinking to myself hell yeah! Afraid of what he would do if I said yes, I answered no. Then the doorbell rang, he went into the bedroom. OMG! I looked out of the window. It was my brother coming to pick us up instead of my mother. I answered the door with my clothes torn and scratches on my neck and face. I turned my back to him (so he couldn't see the scratches) and invited him to sit on the couch. I went behind the wall out of Michael's sight and motioned to my brother what had just happened to me. He jumped off the couch and was ready to fight, but I said to him, "No, let's go." I gathered just enough clothes for me and the children for that day, and as we were about to leave the house I looked down the hall I saw Michael sitting on the edge of the bed swallowing a hand full of pills. He immediately started to gag and vomit. I looked at him, turned my head and finally got the courage to walk out the door. A few hours later I received a call from the hospital asking me if I knew Michael and that he was asking for me. They asked if I would come to the hospital and my response was "Absolutely not! Pump his stomach, he just swallowed a hand full of pills and called for an ambulance himself. No ma'am, I am not coming!" It was another trick to pull me back into his web again. He was a coward, and too afraid to kill himself. It was another one of his manipulation tactics to get me to do what he wanted.

For seven months Michael called begging for me to come home and promising that He would never hit me again or treat me that way again. He promised he'd changed and all that was important to him was his family. All I ever had before me was a family image. My parents provided that well and that's what I wanted. My vision of family was real but my reality was distorted. He painted a picture of worlds that went along with my vision of family and I went for it. I was finally convinced and on the eight month, we went back.

Chapter 3 – Living Through It

Over the next two years Michael kept his word for the most part. The physical abuse stopped but that monster called jealousy and envy appeared frequently. He wanted another child in the midst of it all but that was unthinkable to me. I made sure to pop those birth control pills like I was eating tic tacs. I remember taking a trip with my mother and when it was time to take my birth control pill, I realized that the new pack of birth control pills were not in my purse. Needless to say that Michael had taken them. He always said that we should be fruitful and multiply, like the bible says. After arriving back home from my trip with my mother and of course after seven days of being away, sex was on his mind. A few months later, I found out that I was pregnant. Oh my God!

We decided to move into a house that my parents owned. I was beginning to feel good again; not feeling like a caged animal. I was two houses down from my parents and now I could see friends that I grew up with. I wasn't making any major moves, still didn't go far, but felt I had a little more freedom. Sitting on the front porch was like strolling through the park on a bright and sunny day. One particular day, I was sitting on the porch and a neighbor spoke to me as he did every day. There was no conversation, just a simple exchange in hellos. I made sure of that. I was determined that my visits to the front porch would not turn into ammunition for Michael. Once he heard the neighbor's hello, he ran out the house to the porch and shouted with such anger "So he's asking for your number now"! I softly said "He just said hello". "So now he's speaking to you" he shouted. I got up and walked down to my mother's house and said to myself "Michael is crazy. He's starting up again, I can't continue in this mess with him."

After a few hours later, I returned home. OMG! What in hell was loosed! Jealousy and anger had taken over him. He walked the floor all night accusing me of the worst things. He wouldn't allow me to sleep and when he did, I'd awake to him standing over me as if he wanted to kill me. This went on for days. It got so bad that I began sleeping with a pair scissors under my pillow. I didn't know what I would see when I opened my eyes. He continued this day and night. It was torture. My children were old enough to know that daddy was angry all the time and they kept asking why he was mad. Michael would get in my face, point his finger and say "I know you are doing something, you can't fool me!" He could never tell me anything specific that I was doing, just talking foolishly.

I remember another day when Michael went to work. My girlfriend Linda called me and said she was in town. I thought it would be a good idea to see her since she came all the way from California to visit some relatives nearby. So I invited her over. We are reminiscing, laughing and enjoying each other's company when Michael burst through the door. He didn't speak or anything, just walked right passed us and all of a sudden, we saw the phone being dragged across the floor. We looked at each other and said, did that just happen? My girlfriend looked at me and said "It's time to go." After she left, I walked into the bedroom where Michael was and asked "What was that all about? He didn't answer right away, but then I heard the pitter patter of my baby daughter's tiny feet running as fast as her little legs could carry her. She entered the room with all the zeal and excitement that a daddy's girl could have and he said to her as if he was talking to an old hunting buddy, "Baby girl, daddy just bought a gun". I thought "OMG!!" "That's it for me."

Chapter 4 – The Escape

The thought of this unstable man having a gun in his possession was unbearable. The decision to leave happened that day. The jealously and rage he showed was so intense. I knew deep inside of me that if he ever got a chance, he would pull that gun on me and use it. He'd already told me that he would kill me. He said "If I can't have you nobody will!" That day I took the 2nd car, my kids and left to move in with my parents. The next day, I realized that we didn't have any clothes so I waited until it was time for Michael to go to work to return to the house. All the while I was there I had a bad feeling. There was a noise coming from the back of the house, so I took what I grabbed and went out the front door. Later that night I asked my brother, my dad, and best friend to go back with me. They didn't feel good about being there either so we hurried and left. Later we found out that Michael was there hiding inside the closet. He was listening and watching us, waiting on the right moment to make his move. He was surprised we left so quickly.

A week later, all hell broke loose! I finally got a job; this was the first day actually. The position was a cashier at an elementary school cafeteria. I was so excited to have some independence. My mother, father and brothers had left for work. It was about 8:00 a.m. I would report at 10:00a.m. I was getting ready for work, my two older kids were gone to school and the baby girl had her run of the house. The doorbell rang. I peeped out the window and low and behold it was Michael. He was supposed to be at work. He shouted "I need to get something out of the trunk!" I believed him and I had the only key to that car. We went to the car to open the trunk when all of a sudden he pulled out a gun! He told me to get in the car! All I could think of was my baby girl standing there looking as she stood between us. I did just as he told me all the while I was looking down the barrel of a gun. I was praying all the time that the car wouldn't start and bless God, it didn't. He snatched me out of the car and tried to start it himself, but it wouldn't.

He jumped out the car still holding me at gun point and ordered me into the house. He pushed me inside and slammed the door. He ordered me upstairs and began pushing me up the stairs. Once we were up the stairs, he told me to take off all my clothes. I prayed that God would create an escape for me. Immediately it sounded like a door closed so Michael ran to the window to see what's going on. That was it, my way of escape. I grabbed my baby and ran down the stairs. As I opened the door to run out, Michael caught up with me and snatched me back in. I screamed as loud as I could and I saw my neighbors running out the door. Everything was in slow motion. He slammed the door all the while holding the gun. BANG! The gun goes off and smoke was everywhere. I couldn't tell if I was shot, my baby was shot or what exactly was going on. Michael had taken the baby at that time so I looked hard at her for blood. I didn't see anything. I didn't feel anything or see any blood so that cleared us. Then all of a sudden, Michael shouted "Look what you made me do!" He had shot himself in the foot! He then said in an evil tone "If I can't have you, nobody will!"

Now that he's hurt, things get more intense. He pushed me to the back door. I immediately took my baby from him and told him "You will not take my child! We walked between the houses, through the rain, mud and rocks and the up the alley to his car. He told me to get in, but I wouldn't. I knew if I got in that car, I was dead. Refusing to get in, I held tightly to my baby with one arm while pushing against the car door with the other. I had to fight with everything within me not to get into that car.

Being shot in the foot Michael realized this was not working. He got in the car and just as he was changing his tactics, I saw another split moment to get away. I ran to the other side of the car still holding my baby. He put the car in reverse, I went in reverse too. He moved the car forward, I moved forward also. He then put the gun on the passenger side of the front seat and I began to run. BANG! BANG! BANG! Michael was unloading the gun at me. I could hear bullets passing by my head. Then all of a sudden BOOM! I was hit, shot in the back! The bullet dislocated my shoulder. Mind you, I was hit on the side that I was carrying my baby while running. I had to put my baby down as I was in so much pain and I wanted to see if the bullet went through my shoulder and reached my little one. I put her down, she was ok, but I was bleeding profusely. I couldn't pick her back up but told her to run with mommy. She was crying, I was screaming! I ran between the houses and through the mud. I wasn't sure if my baby was still following me, I was trying to get some help. While holding my dislocated shoulder, I had to now jump a four-foot fence while dodging bullets in order to reach my neighbor. The fence ripped my pants and tore my flesh wide open. With a bullet in my back, a dislocated shoulder, and torn flesh, I had no choice but to keep moving. I ran down the neighbor's driveway. When I reached the end of the driveway, a neighbor pulled me to her. All I could think of was my child. "I have to get my child; I have to get my child!" She comforted me by saying "The child is okay, my daughter has her." I was in so much pain and my body felt as though it was on fire. I couldn't tell if I was hit more than once. The police and paramedics arrived almost immediately. They examined me and were curious about where all the blood was coming from. My clothes were completely soaked in blood. I could hear someone say "She's been shot." They couldn't tell where the bullet exited my body. God had spared my life and the life of my baby.

I was rushed to the hospital in an ambulance and was treated immediately. I was told that the bullet entered through my back and ricocheted off my right shoulder blade, tore through the nerves in my shoulder where it stopped just underneath the last layer of skin. The doctors said if they operated, there would be a 50/50 chance that I would never use my right arm again. I decided to have the surgery and believe God to do the rest. The pain was excruciating but I was determined to have full use of my right arm. The 12 weeks of physical therapy was painful and exhausting. All I could think of is "I've got to live through this!

I received great spiritual and physical support. My Pastor came and prayed with me and the church took good care of me. God had indeed spared my life and now I was even more determined to live for Him.

Chapter 5 – Enough

By now you would think I have been through enough. After that last ordeal with Michael, I was through. Michael was arrested and it was time to go to court. All of that in itself was a miracle. I didn't really want to go to court because I didn't care to see him again, ever! I found out that Michael was previously married and had done similar things to his first wife. She was at court and more than happy to testify. Her testimony was so horrific that I didn't even have to get on the witness stand. Michael went to jail immediately. I filed for divorce, but he wasn't in the divorce granting mood. That didn't matter, I had enough! A divorce was what I wanted and a divorce was what I was going to get. Everything that everyone said during and after the wedding made sense now. If I had only known! If I had only asked.

After the divorce process, I had sworn off men. I didn't want to date, be introduced to anyone, or meet anyone – period. A girl friend of mine invited me over for an evening out. She didn't tell me that there would be someone there she wanted me to meet. In walks this handsome man that not only catches my eye, but made me look twice. All I could say was "humm". She immediately gets him, bring him over and introduces him as Bobby. I was determined not to be kind, or look interested, but his voice was captivating and just as smooth as he was beautiful. I convinced myself not to get caught up in the conversation that night and I left with my pride intact and confident. I didn't give in and I was quite proud of myself.

The next day my phone rang; it was Bobby. My girlfriend had given him my number and told him to call. He convinced me to meet him for dinner, which was, by the way, very pleasant and he told me a little about his story. He was a gentleman, very kind, smooth, and wanted a family. As we dated, I began looking for something to go wrong. We had normal dating issues like everyone else does. It was nothing, so I thought.

Time passed by and it was time to spend Christmas with his family. I knew he was going to propose, I executed plans to distract him. He didn't ask me that day. Later on, we went to dinner and he finally proposed. I said yes and we were married at my church home.

The marriage was good. Bobby would take us on family trips and we would spend quality time together as a family. After about 2 years, things started to change. His time became an issue; hours at home were far and few between. He started spending time at the local bootleg house; as a result, drinking and gambling were becoming his priorities. He stopped paying the bills. I remember coming home one day and the power was turned off. That was a long, cold winter. He would blame me because of the way things were. I would look for certain items in the house but couldn't find them. It was later revealed that he was pawning them.

The drinking became frequent. There was no physical abuse, but my God, the verbal and mental abuse was unbearable. He called me all kinds of names and told me I was nothing. He convinced me that if I left him, no one would want me. I was caught between two minds. My ex-husband because of his own insecurities thought every man walking wanted me and this one, was telling me that no man would want me. I didn't know what to think. Then I had enough! I took all I could take of being verbally abused. His words struck me hard, blow after blow. He might as well have beaten me with his fist. One night after the drinking and throwing insults, he fell asleep. I waited patiently to make sure he was in a deep sleep. He was about to get a taste of a real mad black woman. I knew I wouldn't hurt him physically so I got the scissors and began to cut up his clothes. Not the ones hanging in the closet, but the ones he had on his back. I cut them to shreds, every piece; even his underwear. I didn't care if he knew what had happened to him when he woke up the next morning or not. The next morning, I got up and sat on the edge of the bed waiting for him to wake up. When he did, he stood on his feet and every shred of clothing fell to the floor. Some pieces were still in the bed. That's not all I did, I painted his toe nails red, put liquid paper in his mustache and put his hair in rubber bands. It was so hard to keep the laughter in, but on the inside, I was laughing my butt off! He didn't say a word. Not even when he went to the bathroom and looked in the mirror. Now he was confused. I would catch him looking at me as if he wondered why in hell did she do this.

Another time when I was feeling myself was when I came home one day and couldn't see the ground for negros' feet. Bobby had a yard full of his buddies, male and female, in the front year yard having a barbeque. People and smoke was everywhere. I got mad on the spot; pulled up, jumped out of the car and didn't say anything to anyone. Speaking to myself, "Not today!" I went into the kitchen, grabbed a pan, walked back outside, lifted the lid on the grill and started putting all the chicken, ribs and corn in the pan. It didn't matter whether it was done or not. By the time all the smoke from the grill had evaporated, all the meat was in the pan. I grabbed the water hose and put the fire out! When I looked up, all the people were gone! Bobby couldn't say anything. He was in a state of shock.

Things didn't get any better and for my own sake and the sake of my children, I knew things had to change. He came home drunk again and this time for me it was over. When he went to work the next day, I had all the locks changed. He came home drunk again, staggering and singing. He tried to use his key to get in. He didn't know whether he was using the right key or just couldn't get the key to fit in the key hole. Eventually, he started yelling for me to open the door. I never did, he slept on the front porch that night. The next day, he tried again to open the door and couldn't. Then the cussing started and the yelling. He realized I had the locks changed. I stood my ground and this time, I told him he had to leave. I had taken all I was going to take. He left, but it wasn't quietly. He tried for the next six months to come back, but I wouldn't allow him to. I eventually filed for divorce, and he granted it.

During that 6-month period, Eric had come home from the military and stopped by to see his son. I was getting ready to go to work when the car wouldn't start. He offered me a ride and I took it. As we were pulling off, I noticed in the rear that we were being followed by Bobby. I immediately let Eric know as I didn't want to drag him into my mess. I told him that Bobby was going to call me once I got inside, and he did. I told him that the marriage was over and that I had filed for divorce. This made Eric a little more comfortable in his pursuit and the chase was on!

Eric came around more often and attended to me and the children. He was a good man and I realized he was the one for me all along. He wasn't perfect, but he was a good man! After 11 years his love for me hadn't changed. In fact, he said the only reason he got married was because I started dating Michael. He married because I had hurt him not because of love. I could understand how he felt and what he was saying because I felt the same way. After all, we were each other's first love.

Chapter 6 – Returning to my First Love

Eric had the green light. The pursuit was on and he was relentless. He would cook for us and there was nothing that he didn't do for me and the children. He really won me over when he cooked my favorite meal for me one evening. He went through so much to set the atmosphere with dimmed lights, candles on the dinner table, soft music...the works! He didn't bother with wine because he knew I couldn't hold my liquor nor did I like the taste. He had another plan...a wine cooler. It was sweet, cool and not hard, just right for me. The evening was beautiful until I finished that wine cooler. Apparently, it had more alcohol in it than we thought. I was high as a kite. Eric didn't know what to do. All of a sudden, a Patti Labelle song came on and you would have thought I was her! Singing at the top of my lungs and swaying to the music showed Eric a side of me that he thought was hilarious! I was still aware of what was going on. He tried to slow dance but I knew he would have had me for real; it was time to go. He tried his best to get me to stay, but I told him no. "You can take me home, but you can't stay" I told him waving my finger in his face. He was going to have to work for me; nothing was coming easy.

Eric saw to it that the children and I had what we needed. My family had already included him in the family even though he had not asked to marry me yet. I was sure he wanted to, but he didn't know how. Some of my issues began to resurface; trust issues and insecurities. He had to remind me on several occasions that he wasn't those guys that abused me. He assured me that there was a future with him if I would allow it.

As time went by, I got more comfortable with him and I saw that I could actually depend on him for everything. Then one day as I was ironing, Eric came up behind me and said "Are you going to marry me?" The kids thought that was hilarious and told him, "You can't ask her to marry you like that; you're supposed to get on one knee." And so he did, on one knee he went and asked me to be his wife. It was easy for me to answer right away because he had stolen my heart a long time ago and was now reclaiming it. I immediately said yes.

We discussed a date and called the church for counsel. We had a private ceremony at the church. This time it would be forever. Now there were times when we wanted to throw each other out the front door like the time I painted his toe nails and took a picture of it. It took him two days to get all that red polish off his feet. Or the time he cooked a pot of chitterlings and I wanted to put him and the pot out the back door! There was a time about a year into the marriage when Eric worked security. My insecurities spoke to me and said he was doing something else. I decided to find out. I went to the beauty supply store and purchased a wig and a pair of sun glasses. I tricked him into telling me where he was working and showed up in disguise. Sitting there I watched him as he worked for hours until it was almost time for Eric to get off. At that point, I rushed home.

Eric and I like to have fun; we travel together, worship together, and work together. We can tell when we've had enough togetherness and we call each other out on it. We run our individual errands or make our individual appointments just to get some alone time. It works for us.

There were times when I thought of getting a divorce, but we worked things out. I was stressed and had a lot of things on my plate. It was me, nothing he could do was right until he began to point out my flaws. That made me take another look at myself and, with a little counsel, I made the adjustments. I would find myself reverting, placing blame or not showing trust. All he would say is "**My name is Eric**." Enough said.

We recently went on a couple's retreat and of all the people they called Eric and I up to say something. The question that was addressed to Eric was "If your spouse could grant you one wish, what would it be?" Eric cleared his throat and said "longevity". The room was silent. Then the sobbing began and not a dry eye was left in the place. I immediately began to think, "Wow", where did that answer come from. Was it because all of my previous relationships were short lived? Could it be that he was reflecting on our courtship in our earlier years? That spoke volumes to me. Eric would usually have some comedic answer, or filibuster, but not this time. He said longevity because he loves me. And that he enjoys spending time with me. He loves being in my presence. Time away he says is time wasted. I couldn't believe it. He said the right thing. I was speechless. I couldn't say a thing. That did it for me. My eyes, like everyone else's, were filled with tears. At that moment, I realized everything that I needed was standing right there beside me, ready to give his all and willing to live through it too!

So now, am I angry? Am I sad? No. This experience gave me a story. I had to live through it in order to tell it. To be a witness of God's amazing Grace is the height of my testimony.

Chapter 7 – Facing My Issues

I never dealt with my issues, I escaped them twice. When I packed my bags to leave, the issues were packed too; it was a suitcase of issues. I eventually realized that running from bad situations only cause you to live to face them along the way. In order to move forward you have to come to grips with your part of any issue or you will repeat it all over again. You might find yourself looking for the same thing or acting out in similar manner. It's easy to place all the blame on someone else but you're only fooling yourself. The older generation said it best "To thine own self, be true".

The Retaliation

I didn't realize that I had slipped into retaliation mode until I began writing this book. It shocked me that I could act so out of character. While trying to figure that out, I realized that retaliation came because of unforgiveness. I hadn't forgiven the two husbands mentioned in my previous relationships.

Michael

Even in the worse situation with Michael retaliation came. The day he took the pills and began to vomit I retaliated by looking at him, turning my head and walking out the door. He would be okay, and I refused to stay to help and clean up that mess. It was his, let him clean it up! I even thought that I should do something to get rid of him because I knew that he was going to get rid of me. This was totally out of character for me, but things had gotten just that bad. All types of crazy thoughts were developing. Although they flooded my mind I could never go through with any of them. It's amazing to think how you allow someone to push you so close to the edge. Had I followed my mind, I would be locked up somewhere behind bars or on a special floor with padded walls. Thank God for a sound mind!

Bobby

Throughout all the mind games and belittlement, I never thought about retaliating until I had enough. Knowing that Bobby wouldn't remember what happened to him because he was drunk, I began to play little games too. I didn't do any physical harm to him but because of unforgiveness, I began to play the mental games and said "Let him figure that out!"

Being in either situation wasn't good. You don't repay evil with evil, but rather overcome evil with good. I just couldn't see it at that time. Now that the smoke has cleared and the memories are not suppressed, I realize the state I was in. Of course, I've repented of those actions and can now deal with my issues (some) face on.

Eric

Eric has no problem "calling me out" when I doubt him or am hesitant and put him in the same category as my two previous husbands. He says "I'm not them!" "Whatever the issue is, we can work it out; we're not leaving each other". I can appreciate that. He's proven that he is willing to work together and face our issues head on. It's not always the easiest thing to do, but I am walking it through.

Pam

Now this is the hardest person to deal with, me. I know the thoughts that creep at night; the overwhelming feelings that occasionally sweep over me and the feelings of insecurities that resurface. To overcome them, I have to keep myself encouraged in the Word of God, daily confessions and prayer. I look forward to the gentle, quiet voice of the Holy Spirit of God speaking directly to my spirit calming me and giving me peace like no other. This is my testimony; there is a place in God where the enemy can't touch you, where nothing else matters or what no one else thinks.

I have realized that I have to face my issues, pray about them or talk to someone about them or else I will find myself in the same position as before…a state of unforgiveness! That is not the place for me.

www.ingramcontent.com/pod-product-compliance
Lightning Source LLC
Chambersburg PA
CBHW021123020426

42331CB00004B/601